Drawing to Extinction

Poems and Pictures
by
Pat Arrowsmith

HEARING EYE

HEARING EYE
99 Torriano Avenue,
London,
NW5 2RX

ISBN 1 870841 73 5

This publication has been made possible with the financial
assistance of the London Arts Board.

Printed by Catford Print Centre
Typeset by Daniel James at mondo designo

Previous poetry publications (plus pictures) by Pat Arrowsmith:
Nine Lives (Brentham Press), *On the Brink* (CND), *Thin Ice* (London
CND), *Breakout* (Edinburgh University Student Publications Board)

Fiction:
Jericho (Cresset Press and GMP), *Somewhere Like This* (WH Allen,
Panther and GMP), *The Prisoner* (Journeyman Press), *Many Are
Called* (Onlywomen Press).

Memoir-cum-fiction:
I Should Have Been a Hornby Train (GMP).

Non-fiction:
To Asia in Peace (Sidgwick and Jackson), *The Colour of Six Schools*
(Society of Friends Race Relations Committee).

POEMS

PICTURES

ACKNOWLEDGMENTS

Journals in which poems and pictures have been previously published include:
Poetry Monthly, Tribune, Peace News, Vole, Between the Lines, Ver Poets' Collections, *Pennine Platform, Socialist.*

Some have been included in the following books:
The West in her Eye (Pyramid Poetry), *Work* (Katabasis), *Ver Poets' Voices* (Brentham).

For my Niece Hilary

GETTING OLD

I may get alzheimered,
Brain shrivelled into second childhood.
I may seize up,
Need new joints and ear-drums.
My teeth may crumble,
Eye-lens get befogged.
Or spawning cells gone wild
May slowly strangulate
My bowel and lungs and liver.

All this may happen, or may not.
Certainly, curtains will grow ragged,
Gas-stove start to smell,
TV, record-player get erratic.

And I shall start to ponder:
Will they last me out?
Good, not many years to go now.
I may not need to buy replacements,
Repaint the bathroom walls;

Nor with any luck be forced to struggle
With baffling new contrivances:
Computer-managed kitchen, shopping;
Fax, internet and complex phones.

Advancing years will let me off the hook.
Allow me to forget names, past events;
And not to worry—must I really do those things?—
Accept my skin is wrinkled, hair turned grey.

Yes, I'm glad I'm getting on.
Am past the time for facing certain crises.
Dire pre-old age diseases,
Personal calamities.

And, who knows,
I might be old enough by now
To avoid the environmental cataclysm,
Miss the nuclear holocaust
That may await us all.

ADVENTURE IN IRAQ
(after taking part in the Gulf Peace Camp)

It wasn't real desert:
no undulating dunes,
picture postcard camels,
sand;
only pariah dogs, cats, grit and
stones.

It wasn't the scorching weather
we'd expected,
but rain, wind, icy nights.
'I'd rather be killed than cold'
I often said.

He wasn't a real monk
despite the Buddhist robe
he sometimes sported.
Chicago priest donned casual clothes;
she, a US nun, wore slacks.

We weren't in a real war zone
liable to blaze in flames,
but miles away from any town,
in a sort of Spartan Butlins

that wasn't a real camp:
tents sheltered beneath roofing;
cooking done in kitchen shed;
even taps and sketchy toilets
more or less supplied.

Nor did it seem a real war:
no shells, artillery or tanks;
no fighting over our dead bodies;
only passing bombers' roar.

It wasn't quite a real air raid:
no throb of aircraft,
searchlights,
ear-splitting explosions;
just pretty fireworks in the sky.

Nor were we the real heroes
('named in gold in Iraq's history')
that They said we were,
but merely forced evacuees,
Their prime concern our safety.

We weren't really a peace group at all:
arguing at endless meetings,
riven by factions,
deep suspicions—
people often full of hate.

Yet for the first time in my life
I lived entirely in the present;
past irrelevant;
future quite obscure.

And now it's over and I'm back
nothing seems quite real any more.

12.2.91

HERCULES BOUND

(Hercules was a bear used in TV commercials who escaped in Scotland for a time)

Oh Hercules
I grieve, grieve.
You swam to freedom.
Why did they have to retrieve
you, not let you prowl at liberty
among the Hebrides
over moors and fells?—
your fur braced cool, blown wild
by winds, the breeze
brightening your feral eyes,
your strong paws furrowing the seas.

And God created great whales
(and bears and seals)
and saw that it was good.
Never never did She mean
such splendid creatures to cower on their knees,
posture on television screen
to promote the sale of processed cheese
and chemically made honey.

Oh Hercules
I grieve, as She must grieve,
who didn't create teddy-bears,
whales for pet-food;
but real bears, real whales,
real Eve.

LOVE POEM

I stare at the mirror,
at the pond surface,
and realize at last
what love is not.

It is not glittering stream
swirling round boulders,
cascading in foam,
sunspray dazzling;

or crash of breaker
on shelving seashore,
mouthing shingle,
sucking one under.

It is not rush of blood,
lurch in the loins,
libidinous juice
hectically surging;

or my own frenzied face
in ecstasy, agony,
staring back at me,
seeing no one else.

No, it's you whom at last
I see in the mirror—
your eyes, expression,
not mine for a change.

May your image not blur,
or reflection cloud over.
May the glass stay intact
and your face remain.

COAL

Coal:
jet jewels,
bright faceted fuel
whose fired radiance
ejects no secret atom shafts
to poison penetrate its users;
smouldered red in homely grate;
glowed orange in kitchen range;
can safely power manufacture.
Its dark caverns shine
deep down underground
waiting to be mined
for hidden
treasure.

FRIENDSHIP

Friendship—
an entity
of great fragility:
two glass bubbles;
a puff
and they touch;
but the least gust
and they clash,
burst,
are shattered
to infinity.

POOL
(prescient poem written in early 1968)

Clatter,
clack, tack, whack,
racking, sack, cack
go the keys.
Clatter of crisp typists' court shoes trimly
stepping out down corridors,
along the aisles to
their desks.
Clack of their voices,
up, down, prim, shrill, hushed with
trivial excitement,
in the tea-break,
in the canteen,
in the toilet.
Their fingers, eyes, tack this way and that
all morning;
all afternoon;
evening overtime if possible;
letters to invoices to envelopes to forms to
invoices to envelopes to forms to letters to
envelopes to letters to forms to invoices...
Whacked,
racked with clockwork tension by 5.15 pm:
cramped knees,
numbed buttocks,
squint eyes,
taut neck rusted on aching shoulders,
finger-joints strained with stumbled racing
for what?—
next day, the sack.

No more clack of voices,
heel clatter,
fingers tacking till whacked,
racked with exhaustion;
but:
'Thank you very much Miss Smith, and
we hope you soon find suitable
alternative employment.'
For the pool's turned electronic:
thought waves from machine brains
tap the keys,
type the invoices,
copy the letters,
fill the forms,
stamp the envelopes.
Typists, clerks, stenographers
now are so much
cack.

CREATION
(concerning the potential fate of
pit bull terriers a few years ago)

Man (sic) made God in his own image—
a killer—
took a dislike to him
and killed him;
then made dogs in his own image—
turned them into killers—
took a dislike to them
and planned to kill them...

DAVID AND GOLIATH
(the launch of a space probing rocket was delayed because woodpeckers punctured its metal casing)

Moth frail hang-gliders
Breeze buoyed up in hot air hovering;
Or lightly motorized,
Like buzzing insects,
Clockwork toys
Piloted the simple way.

I am conservative—
Hate and fear sound-barrier breaking aircraft,
The rush and roar of Channel Tunnel trains,
Bewildering electronic networks,
Computer driven artificial worlds.

But I would praise and decorate
Those cheeky, metal puncturing woodpeckers
Who sabotaged a hypercomplex rocket
Aiming to probe, explore the universe.

For while we endlessly design
Ever more intricate artifacts and engines
We revere, appear to hanker after nature
And the primitive devices once employed
Decades, centuries ago.

SELF VIEW
(after being interviewed on television)

This person seems effective:
controlled, articulate, unruffled;
able to pause and think, consider,
‚look pensive, give unhurried answers,
smile at times, even appear light-hearted,
reply to every question in a reasoned manner.

I quite like her, quite approve—
we'd probably get on quite well together,
find a fair amount in common, have discussions,
respect each other, share a joke.

But surely we have met already?
There's something faintly, puzzlingly familiar
about her hair-style, general cast of features.
This person cannot be a complete stranger.

On second thoughts, she is—she just resembles
someone I once saw or met or knew,
noticed in a shop or on the underground.
And yet...

"That went well, flowed smoothly, was provocative;
must have stimulated audience reaction.
Thank you very much indeed for coming.
It really was a lively, gripping interview..."

So that was it—was why I felt I'd met her:
that fluent, relaxed woman whose words I'd hung on,
wondering how she'd deal with every question,
impossibly, incredibly was me.

AFTER INVADING COULPORT
(Trident's storage site)

Ethereal but ephemeral pale blue,
rose-tinged ochre touched with film of mauve,
Scottish hills one hazy sun-shone day.

Undulating, peaking here and there.
Sloping gracefully, fading gradually
in the calm, summer-still October air.

Yet it is autumn.
Our carefully modulated cerebral nerves
gently slanting, curving, towards wise deeds
are jarred with sudden angles,
pocked with pot-holes.
Beside the quiet tracks, unlooked-for chasms;
dark burrows;
unstable unexpected rock seams;
volcanic faults
dynamited with untimely thunder, lightning;
winter storms in store.

This mountain body laid before us,
overlaying us,
starkly skeletoned within us
is porous, penetrated through and through
with poisoned veins,
lethal warren of capillaries.

But we can block their entries;
extract and drain their venom;
straighten jagged nerves, contorted arteries;
stanch deadly fluids;
if we will,
stifle thunder;
extinguish lightning;

stave off non-inevitable,
not ineluctable,
nerveless, boneless,
shapeless, colourless,
barren, starving,
final, freezing,
never ending,
cataclysmic,
nuclear winter.

GUY FAWKES NIGHT

Stellar parasol bursts open,
Stretches through the night towards us,
Galaxy of coloured sparks
That crackle in the dark above.

Strange, festive way to mark a killing
Committed centuries ago—
A curiously innocent display,
Or mainly so.

Better than exploding rockets
That spread a zillion nuclear spores
Invisibly, insidiously,
Gradually or suddenly
Making corpses of us all.

DINNER HOUR ON THE OFFICE ROOF

Almost in the clouds,
I feel remote, cool, uninvolved.
Those hectic people in the offices below
are strangers.
Their chatter, comings, goings, flurry
are no concern of mine.

A stiff breeze lifts my hair,
sweeps my skin so freshly
that I do not notice the soot specks
carried in its current.
And from this windy height
the packed traffic,
swarming, crawling crossly
through the streets below
is merely the faint roar
of breakers on a distant beach.

I stare at the rugged panorama:
brick and window-pane checked walls
tower up.
Masonry, red and yellow chimneys
crag the skyline.
Office-block, shop, factory cliffs
surround me,
their ledges, patchwork terracing of rooftops
spread about below.

I have escaped:
am no longer in the city
but in some wild, solitary place
where the wind throws shadows on the rock face.

For one quiet hour I am on my own,
far away,
at liberty,
free from them all,
free from myself,
free even from you.

THE NEW WORLD ORDER—
SOLDIERS ARE STILL STRUTTING

Holocaust containers turned to foil,
globe-exploding contents dispersed,
venom dissipated,
yet tiny tinny soldiers are still strutting—
we still haven't learned.

For in our veins battles are still raging,
corpuscular toy soldiers waging wars;
and in our brains aggressive impulses
persist in mustering, forming fours
at the junctions of our neuron tracks.
Glands too are still secreting
corrosive acid, poison, lethal fluid.
Our blood-stream, nervous, endocrinal systems
remain turbulent with pugilistic waves
ridden by tin soldiers, who almost everywhere—
in the Balkans, Middle East, Somalia—
still surge to battles,
serious, savage, yet their causes trivial.

Is it hopeless?
Is slaughter-urge inherent in our nature,
intrinsic to our fabric?
Or could we reconstruct ourselves,
change ourselves,
change our ways of changing things
before it is too late and once again
we face erasure of our world?

20.1.92

DISCORD IN DOVELAND

Marbled wings folded above delicate pink claws;
Neck gleaming with a mauvish emerald sheen;
Nut-button-studded little head,
Poking, peering this way and that;
Soft, solid, blue-grey body
Ruddered by stiff-plumed, flight-fanned tail;
Chest swelling plumply in and out
With urgent, huskily throbbing dove-speech.

You seem the quintessential peace-bird.
But are you really?
For you are much like us,
Human would-be peacemakers—
Your gentle billing all mixed up
With jealousy, assertive rage;
Your vigorously demanding coo
A strutting show of sexual claim,
Display of territorial aggression.

In a frenzied feather-fraught affray
You vanquish fellow-doves,
Expel them from the bird-table.
Then in frustration, frightened anger,
Try to smite my grain-filled palm
With fiercely outspread wing-flap.

Perhaps no one living on this planet—
Beetle, bison, pigeon, human—
Can live in harmony with fellow-beings.
Wrath, fear, envy may it seems
Be common to us all;
Violence, warfare and destruction,
The doom awaiting every creature.

24

WELCOME CALLERS

Pigeon arabesque,
Kinetic sculpture of frenetic wings—
Billowing yacht sails flapping flaglike
As they jostle, squabble,
On the seed-strewn table.

Or peace-doves they may squat
Drowsily meek under my cupped hand,
Lids slowly shuttering sleepy little eyes,
Necks bowed,
Heads drooping down in semi-slumber.

Sometimes lively, playful,
Their beaks point up to be caressed,
Or strain to poke and rub between my fingers,
Gently pecking them
In cheeky pigeon greeting.

I am sixty-three,
Without partner, children, cat or dog;
So these regular dove visitors,
Unhouse-trained,
Noisily demanding though they be,
Are much loved welcome callers;
Have become quite special
And among my closest friends.

18.10.93

POLAR POEM
(After visiting Iceland and Greenland)

Blade-edged chunks snapped off great glaciers,
frozen continents and oceans
blockade the fjords with massive pack-ice,
towering icebergs,
and threaten shipping, coastlines;

while rumbling under planet's crust
explosive power accumulates,
prepares to burst through mountain summits,
rupture ice-caps,
blast whole islands,
pour down streams of molten stone
to drown, burn, totally demolish
homesteads,
hamlets,
townships
in exterminating red-hot torrents.

And Hades chuckles—
a menace of volcanic cauldrons
bubbling with infernal mud.
Geysers suddenly shoot skywards.
Geothermal thunder lies in wait
to tumble buildings,
tear Earth's surface,
crumble cliffs,
hurl huge rocks about.

Yet it is God,
the great creator
(great destroyer),
who plans all this;
so we ourselves are surely made
in His *(sic)* image.

For we too never cease to deal out death;
and we too have in store
such genocidal bomb-blast power
that the nuclear explosions we can detonate
could end all life
and pulverise our globe.

ON NOT BEING A PUSSY-CAT—
EPITAPH FOR ZEYA
(Reflections on the execution
of an imprisoned tiger)

If I were a great bounding cat
with Jung-recall of running wild
whose forebears had been zooed, caged in,
for the fantasies, amusement, whims
of infinitely more vicious beasts
I daresay (pacifist though I am)
I'd pounce upon and rend my guards.
Doubtless I'd be shot for this.
But, who knows, in the end perhaps
I'd be permitted to ascend
to the Valhalla for brave cats.

WINTER WALK

Blank sheet of sky
Above blurred, inspissated foreground.
Pastoral panorama
Blotted out by fleece of mist.
Grey, wraith-tree peopled woodland
Feather pencilled in the dusk.

Then all at once I see
Frigid skeleton of umbellifer,
Silhouetted pale and fragile
Against the twilit coppice,
Straining forward,
Anticipating April,
Pretending icy tracery
Is lacy parasol of spring.

Delicately I touch it.
Frost-stiff fronds are brittle,
Yet solid as a frozen moment
In the concrete present
That is our sole reality:
Crystallised granule of eternity
To be handled carefully
But savoured fully,
Wholly apprehended.

For there may be no flowers next April;
No next spring.

FOR MYRA

Crowned by us with artificial, everlasting horns
Planted firmly on her forehead,
Endeavouring to fall asleep
While strapped upon the nail-thorned mattress
We have placed beneath her
From which she cannot struggle free,
She knows the real horns she certainly once bore
Have vanished now,
Been wrenched out, thrown away by her own self
Exerting all her strength and vigour.

And we too have the seeds of horns
Lodged deep within our skulls, our brains,
Ready to germinate, sprout forth, grow sharp,
That do indeed from time to time thrust out,
Inflicting torture, injury and death.

So should we not have ceased to demonize her:
Denounce, deplore, detest, despise her?
Perhaps it's time we started to admire her,
Horn-free, ever striving Myra.

WOMEN'S POND
(Hampstead Heath)

I swim through liquid foliage,
Enfolded in the pond's reflection,
Engulfed in groves of olive-green,
Wavering strands of fawn and brown,
Patterning the water's depth.

A haven, this, for duck and moorhen;
Pond's glinting surface patched with lily;
Banks rich with bramble-jelly bushes
Densely fringed with ranks of iris.

Haven too from noise and stress,
Suffused with women's peaceful warmth
Where anger melts to friendliness.

Lush and green, still not "developed"
Into some hell of fumes and steel.
Clusters of honeysuckle flourish.
Testosterone is not supreme.

BACH SOLOIST
for Chris

Dusk has fallen;
Silhouette against the twilit window:
Angled geometry of limbs,
Arabesque of arms and shoulder
Sweeps the bow smartly, smoothly,
Across polished wood, taut strings,
Drawing forth spare melody,
Bach's lean counterpoint,
Sculptured cadences and chords.

But there's a price to pay
For crafting this balanced harmony:
Dexterity of fingers, suppleness of wrist
Belie the striving and stretched muscle strain
Repeated day after day again and again,
Producing agonizing pain—
Fate of many violin players.

Impeccable performance,
However great the skill,
Is never easily achieved:
The effort's always hard,
Practice, rehearsing, unremitting,
Sometimes totally disabling—
High cost of expert art.

CAROUSEL
for Freda

Frightening crematorium curtain
Closes off the past for ever,
Totally conceals the future.

So too at airport destination
Carousel screen-drape veils in mystery
What occurred before it was pushed through
By our items of essential baggage—
By us ourselves in fact,
Moving round life's cycle steadily
To the final curtained exit,
Beyond which who can possibly discern
What will or might befall?

Yet surprisingly it all recurs:
(We) our luggage reappears.
Inexorably it re-revolves;
But holdalls, packs, get snatched away,
Or else appallingly do not emerge.

Thus what before had seemed unquestionable,
Logical, following a clear track,
Is after all quite unpredictable,
Not orderly or comprehensible,
As hitherto we had supposed.

CONCEALED SHEDS

Suddenly I glimpsed,
Sunk almost out of sight,
Embedded in massed thorns and shrubs,
Two or three ramshackle sheds—
Run-down railway remnants,
Whose broken-hinged, lopsided doors
Exposed tumble of abandoned sacks
Sinisterly labelled "chemicals" and "I.C.I.";
Whose scuffed, uneven floors,
Littered with rusty rods and twists of tubing,
Barely visible in the half-light,
Would make an all too likely setting
For murderous assault and rape.

Now and then quite unexpectedly,
Prompted by question, scent or melody,
My own submerged sheds stand revealed:
Shells I thought I'd sloughed off long ago,
Unwanted contents totally dissolved—
Those dimly recollected horrors, passions,
Believed for ever lost in distant past.

Not so however:
Past and present are apt disquietingly to merge.
Damaged artifacts and feelings
May sometimes shockingly, abruptly reappear.

THE MASSIVE AND THE MINUSCULE

The massive and the minuscule collaborate,
Collide and coalesce: they don't conflict.
Particles of chromosomes and atoms—
Quarks, protons, genes, electrons—
Facilitate today's dark wizardry,
Bizarre nanotechnology.

And quantum physics joins with knowledge of the infinite
To achieve bewildering new witchcraft.
We can travel light-years faster now than sound;
Observe far reaches of the universe;
Virtually twist time and place around;
Construct freak vegetables and creatures;
Fabricate computer-powered mind.

But beware—
They say the cosmos, starting as a speck
And now expanding seemingly for ever,
Is set to shrink back to a dot.

And don't forget—
A myriad atom fractions can combine
To produce the multi-megaton explosion
That may shatter our hexed planet some doom time
In a thunder-crash of microscopic fragments.

THE BALLAD OF GRUINARD

*(Gruinard is the small island off the
NW coast of Scotland where an anthrax
bomb was tested in World War II)*

Westerly silver shined channel
furrowed we;
breezy isle,
snow coved,
went to see.

Free. Free.

We landed;
bent knee to goddess of
beach, heather, sea;
ascended rocks, upland—
bleak and clean surely?

Then saw offshore
god of war:
bulbous cloud,
shroud of spores
breed nausea,
swollen sores;
store seed of black death
for scores of years,
bleed poison in the soil;
speed slaughter of billions more
than died in war
ever before.

We left that moor,
shore;
took off—
took oar,
fled the horror,
determined to end war;
allow planned plague,
mass poisoning
no more.

HILLTOP VIEW FROM ALEXANDRA PALACE

Spread out beneath me down the slope
Of low, gradually ascending height
I see a quilt of buildings,
Trees, reservoirs, gasometers,
Stitched with lines of road and rail,
Just visible in autumn light.

Elsewhere are Alpine peaks,
Steep, icy Himalayan summits,
All much too lofty and remote
To excite high exaltation.
What lies below cannot be seen—
Valleys, plains, hazed misty white
Are blotted out of sight.

Better to climb the gentler hill,
Uplifted but not unaware
Of all the busyness down there
Than strive to scale the precipice,
Where all you see is distant sky,
Unattainable, up too high.

ASPIRING J-CLOTH

Patch of blue
Kite-like caught surprisingly aloft
In jigsaw counterpoint
Of foliage-thick tree.

How did it arrive?
Gust of wind?
Handiwork of crazy climber?

Why when first I glimpsed it
Did I speculate:
Small polygon of summer sky
Or pretty pale blue flower?—
Till I saw that it was just a J-cloth,
Errant sink utensil,
Trapped unexpectedly up there.

Why did I then expostulate:
Unsightly grubby scrap of litter
Preposterously misplaced!
Back to the scullery at once.
Get it down today.

ABUSE OF POWER

They want to kill you,
These vain, self-important creatures
Who think they are intelligent,
Allowed to dominate and wreck the earth.
They want to kill you.

They want to kill you
If you're badger, bull or fox,
Elephant or salmon.
Just for fun or trophies
They want to torture, tease and slay you;
Hear you yelp, roar, growl and howl;
Watch you struggle, writhe, collapse.
They want to kill you.

They want to kill you
For poaching on their commandeered preserves.
If you occupy or trespass on their territory,
Sully town square with your droppings,
Scavenge their discarded food,
They'll want to kill you.

They want to kill you
If they reckon you have spread disease
They themselves have generated.
In experiments to test new cures,
Or else in order to concoct
Fictitious, horn-primed remedies,
They want to kill you.

They want to kill you
To stock their fridges, stuff their stomachs,
Fabricate fur coats.
And—rodent, reptile, insect, tiger—
If you frighten or harass them
They'll surely want to kill you.

But who are these super-brilliant killers
Who slaughter also their own kind?
These savage beasts are we ourselves.
Perhaps we too should all be killed.

WELFARE AGENCY

Trapped;
Pencil-torch eyes pierce to the bone;
Glazed with benignity their bulbs
Psychograph marrowy tangles of tension.
Rubber-suction smiles pull out hope and pain,
Re-arrange them, set aside
For subsequent inspection.

Trapped;
They must wait there in rows,
Features twisted by drink and debt
Into a raffia-work of worry;
Balloon complexion dented by eyes
Trouble-taut over tummy's load;
Face of crinkled paper
Ripped into four decades' rage
At time's twinges and the callousness
Of grandchildren and daughter-in-law;
Nine-year face of rock
Hung over with pallid seaweed,
Said to have murdered seven kittens
In despair at being forced from home.

Trapped they are, probers and probed;
Tanked, a school of small sword-fish transfixing
Society's burden of flotsam and jetsam;
Yet trapped in a tank of their own designing.

"PROGRESS"...

Science is a two-edged sword:
Millions the world over now get cured
Of disability, disease;
We speed from continent to continent with ease;
Enjoy instant water, light and heat;
Some parched, starving peoples get relief.

Our labs, observatories, computers
Help us discern the bounds of space,
Even a second universe;
Fathom the very source of life,
Ingredients of brain and mind.

But beware, the ultimate disaster
May lie in wait around the corner:
Carelessness, stupidity or greed
May mean we use our graphs, equations,
Observations, calculations
To pollute the Earth; even breed
Cloned monsters who may well displace us;
Decimate countless other species;
Invent diabolical devices
That surely will infect, irradiate,
Slowly poison and debilitate,
Then ineluctably destroy us,
Devastate our fragile planet.

NORTH LONDON GASOMETERS

Across the Palace park,
Beyond the reservoir,
Shining through the sunlit afternoon
Stand a pair of golden crowns
Ringed with filigree—
Two gas-holders, ochre gilded.

Set down amid the streets and railway lines
They contain huge stores of needed comfort:
The energy and glowing warmth
That make our lives worth living.

There are no crowns further down
At King's Cross hub
Where gross development is schemed.

Miniature lake in tiny nature-park
Cowers at the foot of sullen monsters—
Dark gasometers
Towering up and louring down,
Scowling symbols of the modern "progress"
That threatens to tear up our land
And vandalize the world.

For while gasometers occasionally gleam gold,
Too often we see iron.

18.10.94

QUARTETS

Rackets, bows, sweep and flail;
Networks of dodging limbs, of shifting tones,
Intricately interweave.
Movement, sound, stops and starts;
Determined arms rise to perform.
Here on court, and on the stage,
Complex needlecraft of music, sport, is sewn.

On court, two couples run, duck, stretch
In a muscular, staccato pattern;
Battling with agile, tough ferocity,
Bashing and cannon-balling at each other
With the lethal velocity of light.

On stage, four string players unite;
Prolong their notes, pause, escalate;
Counterpoint them in a geometry of sound.
Crescendos resonate, then fade and blend,
Discords resolving into harmony.

Now and again we all play tennis—
Sometimes even violins.

CLIFF-TOP RUIN

Back from knife-shale cliff slicking to the sea
Jagged brickwork rises from deep nettle bank.
Steeped in weeds and ragwort crumbled stone, cement,
Sprout stunted tree-twists—
Masonry and vegetation coalesce.

So do past and present:
This erstwhile farm,
Now a ramble of disjointed walls and chimneys,
Empty window-frames,
Chinked vista-glimpses of the hills behind,
Once housed people—
Raucous farmer, wife and labourers,
Bawling children—
Barking dogs,
Squawking fowls,
Scattering of feral cats.

Seated on a stretch of ragged wall,
Silent in the timeless summer sun
That fixes, photographs the scene,
I can almost hear them:
Ancient spectres of long long ago,
From a time that I can only just recall.

And I wonder why it is these farm remains,
Flanked by collapsed corrugated barn,
Paint-flaked, window-boarded caravan
Sunk in the ground,
Padlocked, long abandoned,
Are older far than ruined castles, tombs,
Abbeys, stately homes or Hadrian's Wall.

Perhaps the shades of what we dimly recollect,
Experienced once upon a time,
In some sense never cease to yearn for,
Are more solid, real, hence much older
Than unknown ghosts from centuries ago.

For a complete list of Hearing
Eye publications, please write
enclosing an SAE to:

Hearing Eye,
Box 1,
99 Torriano Avenue,
London
NW5 2RX

Alternatively, please visit the
Hearing Eye website at:

http://www.torriano.org